New Chapters

By Steve Scovell

"Every soldier hopes for a major battle in his lifetime. This one was mine."

Andy McNab

Phonics, phonics and "foniks"

I started school when I was five. It was an old school with portacabins and a wooden deck outside. There were chairs, too. The toilets were outside. The class was only 30 children, not many! We only did Maths and English. I remember that we did phonics. 'A' for apple, 'B' for bat, 'C' for cat. I used to give up a lot. When the teachers found out that I was struggling to read, they took me out of the class, to learn on my own in a small room. I had to put on headphones and listen to tapes of people reading short books out loud. I couldn't do it. I didn't know how to write what I was hearing. It didn't work. Of course it didn't work.

The school uniform was grey jumpers and grey shorts. It was the same colour as the grey classroom and just as boring too. I didn't like the dinners either. For pudding, we had frogspawn (tapioca) and at break it was a glass of milk. I remember walking two miles to the bus stop every morning, to go to school. Some days were cold, some days warm. I only ever remember walking alone. Later, my mum told me that she used to come with me every single day.

She could've killed me when I told her! I did enjoy playing with the other children, though. That was probably my favourite part. We would play hop, skip and jump and run wild in the school field. When we were told off, we had to stand and face the wall like criminals.

Junior, juicer and junior

I liked junior school, it was fun. I started to learn things, like maths and English, painting and drawing. I can remember joining the school choir too. We would practise singing after school but of course, I wasn't very tuneful. I tried to learn to play the recorder but that only lasted for a year. I don't think that I will be a musician when I grow up. From 10am to 10:30am, we did a lot of running around, 'It' races and football. A lot of football! At school, I was always good at sports like football, cricket and rounders. Anything that involved doing and using my hands, I could do. Anything that involved reading or writing, I couldn't do. I made the school football team, I was the goal keeper. Finally, something I felt that I was good at. Although, I was known to the let the ball through my legs and hit the back of the net every now and then. I played rounders for the school team. I could hit the ball a bloody long way! We won the league one year and got a trophy for the school – it felt like the proudest moment of my life. I HAD ACHIEVED SOMETHING.

Bullies, blows and bunking

My new school was called Swanmore Secondary school. Going to a new school meant meeting a lot of different people, children and teachers. The school was about two and a half miles away from where I lived. We could not afford the bus fare, so I had to ride my bike. My bike was made up of different parts from other scrap bikes at home. It kept on falling apart, so some days, I had to walk to school in all weathers. Most of the other kids had new bikes, so it was no surprise that I never won any bike races.

The lessons that I had at school were:

- English
- French
- Geography
- Maths
- Metalwork
- Music
- RE
- Science
- Technical Drawing
- PE
- Woodwork

The Secondary school was where I had a big problem learning. I was bullied a lot because of my weight and being called thick. That is when I started to fight a lot, nearly every day! I really hated school and

I didn't want to go to school. My parents always told me to go too. Sometimes, I came home and cried because I did not want to be there.

As the years went by, everything became worse. I think that is why I didn't concentrate in lessons or make any effort. Once, I can remember someone was taking the 'mick' out of me and I turned round and punched him. I was sent out of the lesson and given a detention. It was always the same three boys and they were in all my lessons. I never got a break from their teasing. I liked rugby because I could get my own back. I could give them a 'good tackle' and that made me feel better.

My parents did not have much money, but I didn't get free school dinners like at primary school. So, I took sandwiches to school, they were nearly always jam sandwiches. In Year 11, I started to skive off school with a mate. I would leave home, dressed in school uniform and then change and go round to my mates house. We used to collect old used car tyres and sell them for scrap and make a bit of money. Once, I wasn't well and stayed at home. The school attendance lady visited home, to see where I was. She said that she would check that I was in school the next day. Anyway, next day I went to my mates and she turned up checking on my mate and found both of us skiving! That was trouble! I was glad to leave school and didn't take any exams.

Fun, fish and footy

Away from school, I enjoyed several activities with friends. A group of us built a dirt track in a disused chalk pit, where we raced our bikes. I took more risks than the others because I was not worried about damaging my bike, so I regularly won races as long as I did not fall off.

I played football for Bishop Waltham Dynamos, from Under 11-16, in the Eastleigh Minors League. A couple of highlights were:

- Thrashing the unbeaten Waltham Wolves at the Droxford Flower show one year.

- Runners up, one season, in the Eastleigh Minors League, where I started in goal for a while but played most of the season in midfield.

- In our last year, at the end of season, I was voted 'Players' Player of the Season'. I received the trophy from Chris Nicholl, who was playing for the Saints at the time.

For a bit of quiet, I went fishing, which I have always enjoyed. To make a little bit of money, I had paper rounds and on summer weekends I sold strawberries all day in a lay-by for £3.00.

Metal, money and meals

After leaving school, I joined the Youth Opportunities Scheme. I think there were eight of us and we were picked up in a van and taken to where we were working. Our first job was to do up a village hall, painting the walls and varnishing the floor. When we had finished, we went to Bishop Waltham's church and repaired a wall that had been knocked down. After about six months, I went for an interview for a job at a company called Cortursells.

I got the job! The company made wire baskets, like shopping baskets, chip baskets, anything made from wire. After two years, I was offered a welding job, which I took because it paid more. I must have been doing well because they offered to to pay for me to go to college and take a welding course. I said 'No' because there would be too much reading. I worked there for ten years and during that time, I made friends with the foreman and we went fishing a lot together.

My dad then found me a job at Pirelli's in Bishopstoke. It was only a temporary job but I had an interview, so I went dressed in a suit, which surprised the man interviewing me. I was given some tests and I discovered that I was colour-blind. The shifts were twelve hours long, 6 a.m. to 6 p.m., but the pay was very good. The building that I worked in was very long because I was winding long metal cables onto big drums. Eventually the work dried up and it was so boring that I was so pleased to leave, when I was made redundant.

During these jobs, I also had part time jobs. Two that I remember, were the forecourt attendant at a petrol station in the evening and cleaning buses for the day's journeys. This was a bit dodgy, because I started at 3.30 a.m. and the buses were unlocked, so I was always worried if someone was sleeping in them. Finally the place was shut down because there was so much vandalism to them.

This was useful, because after leaving Pirelli's, I worked full time at the petrol station. The shift started at 5 a.m. opening up the garage. At 7 a.m. I went home for breakfast and returned for 10 a.m. till 6p.m. I did this seven days a week, for about fifteen years so I had very little time to myself. The petrol station was very busy and I worked mainly as a cashier.

Eventually, I joined my brother for two years flat roofing. The end came when we fell out and didn't speak to each other for a few years but we have made up and get on together now.

Now I moved to work at a baker's, called Stainer's, in Bishops Waltham. This time, I was working the night shift and it was so repetitive, I hated Easter and all those hot cross buns, I must have baked thousands. If any one was off and they needed a fill in, they would ask me and I couldn't say 'NO'. The work shift was tiring and meant that I met very few people during the day. It was frustrating at work, because it was difficult to pass on information to others. I had to use word of mouth, because I could not write accurately or read instructions. One day, a lady at work , who knew about these problems, told me about Read Easy and encouraged me to contact them. I carried on for another three years but wanted to work fewer hours , so that I had some time to myself and see the sunshine. A lady neighbour told me about Apetito, I applied to them and got the job.

Before I went to Read Easy
Shy, shops and solitude

I was a bit shy and never got involved in going to night clubs or other exciting places. I hated crowds, especially in shops where I was pestered by salespeople and so I would walk out. I never mixed with people of my own age. If I wanted to go shopping, I would ask someone to come with me and bribe them by buying them lunch. I would not drive to large towns without someone with me. Often I would use my mum's catalogue to buy things that I wanted, so I did not have to travel to the shops. If the clothes did not fit, I kept them because I didn't know how to send them back. If I wanted to buy a takeaway, I would park opposite and wait until there were no customers and then I would go in and order. If the takeaway shop never emptied, then I never went in and went home hungry. When I travelled on a bus, I would wait as long as possible for someone else to ring the bell, to get off. I was so nervous about doing things and missed out on so many opportunities to do things.

Discovering Read Easy
Mum, move and meet

When I left school, I started work straight away. I was good with my hands, so all the jobs I did were manual and this suited me because I didn't have to read or write. Most of the time I got people to do things for me, like shopping, Christmas shopping, going fishing or going to the pub. If I had to do things myself, I just put them off or spoke to people rather than fill in forms, like getting car insurance. I knocked around with the same people for years and lived at home until I was 44. My mum helped me get a council flat, where I live now. She also arranged for people to help me to get electricity, gas and phone connections.

It was great to have my own place and I started to do things on my own. It was hard at first and I still relied on people. I met a nice girl at work, her name was Anita. She started to get me out of the house more, we went for meals. She had two black Labradors, called Bella and Sammy and we would take them out for walks a lot. We liked going for walks on the beach at Lee on Solent, where we would relax and eat fish and chips. When I think about the friends that I had before then, I realise that they used me a lot but with Anita it was different. We talked a lot and she helped me a great deal. Once we went on holiday to Ilfracombe in north Devon. Unfortunately, Anita lost her labradors due to old age and that was a sad time for both of us.

One day we were talking and I said that I would love to read a book. She looked on the internet and found a group called Read Easy. She gave me the number to ring but I kept putting it off. This went on for about three weeks and when I next saw her, she said 'Have you phoned Read Easy yet?' and I replied 'No.' Then one day I did phone up and my life started to change. When I called, I spoke to a lady called Pat. I said that I would like to learn to read and write. Pat said that I was the first to phone the group and that it would be a good idea to meet and have a chat. At the end of the chat, we agreed to have a meeting at Tesco's in Winchester and the meeting went very well.

Starting Read Easy
Lorna, bus and book.

I met Pat from Read Easy and we had a chat about reading. She gave me a reading test and when I had completed it, she told me that I had the reading age of a nine-year-old. This made me feel really sad. My next session was with my reading coach, called Lorna. At first, I was a bit nervous but after we had talked for a while, I was much happier. We talked about where we would meet for further lessons and agreed to meet at the Discovery Centre in Winchester, for two half hour meetings a week. For my first lesson, I drove to the Park and Ride, where I caught a bus. It was the first time that I had travelled on a bus for ages and the bus was very busy with lots of passengers. When I reached my stop, I was frightened to press the button, to tell the driver to stop. I waited and waited and luckily someone else pressed the button and I could get off. I walked to the Discovery Centre and waited for Lorna.

When we met, we found a table and had a chat about what we were going to do. Lorna showed me the book that we were going to use, it was called 'Yes, We Can Read'. I started to learn the sounds of the letters and it took me a long time to do this. At home, I started to look on You Tube and watched videos that helped me learn the sounds of the letters. Then we moved on to learning the sounds of pairs of letters and threes of letters. I learnt that these sounds were known as phonics. After learning these sounds, it made reading a little bit easier and I could start to read sentences. I am looking at that book in front of me and now it seems so easy to read, compared to when I was learning to read it.

I started to read more books with Lorna, the first one was called 'Esio Trot'. I read the first page and there was a lot of learning about letter sounds and putting letters together. We soon started to blend the letters together. We started to work together for an hour a week, still catching the bus to the library. I felt a lot more confident catching the bus and pressing the button for my stop.

It was getting close to Christmas and it was getting much busier in town and on the bus. We decided to go to Costa at Tesco, to have our lessons. I was a bit nervous at first, people were sat next to us, at the same table. After a few lessons, I was more confident and didn't worry about the people. At this time, I had an interview with a lady, who was interested about people struggling to read. She asked a lot of questions about how reading had made my life better. At first, I started stuttering because I was a bit nervous but the lady said that the interview had gone well.

Symonds, study and students.

In September 2018, I started to go to the Adult Education Centre at Peter Symonds College in Winchester. The course was one morning a week, from 9.00 a.m. to 1.30 p.m. This was after finishing my night shift at the bakery at 2.30 a.m. I went home had a quick shower and nap for a couple of hours. I would get to college by 7.00 a.m., avoiding the traffic and snooze in the car for a little while.

The course that I was studying was called Level 1 Functional Skills in Reading and Writing. There were many students of different ages, backgrounds and nationalities all wanting to improve their skills for different reasons. We were tested by two written exams, in Reading and Writing. I had never taken an exam before, so John from Read Easy helped me. We met every Monday afternoon for an hour to prepare for the exams.

I also had to give a talk to the group on 'Healthy Eating', which was good for me. I have learnt quite a bit about food preparation and cooking in my jobs. At the end of the course I passed both exams, after retaking the Reading exam. In the exams, I found it difficult to keep track of time. In one exam, I was so pleased that I could do it, that I kept writing and writing. The trouble was that when the examiner said 'you have ten minutes left', I had not started the second question. I freaked and shouted out 'S**t'. Everyone found it funny and I quickly wrote down some bullet points and passed the exam.

At the end of the course, I was really pleased because I had achieved something new. I could write a letter and could communicate with people on paper and by email. This was a big achievement for me and I met new friends. I would have liked to have taken the Level 2 Course, but I could not fit in the time.

My Favourite Books

My three favourite books are:

- 'A dog called Hope' by Damien Lewis.
- 'Today Everything Changes' by Andy McNab.
- 'Mr Stink' by David Williams

'A dog called Hope' is interesting from start to end. It is a story about a bloke called Jason Morgan, who had an accident on a mission in Ecuador and he ended up as a paraplegic. At home, his wife leaves him with their three children. The story is about a dog called Napel, who helps Jason and gives him the help to do many exciting things. The book was good because you want to carry on reading to find out how they succeed together. The story ended with a mixture of sadness and success for Jason.

When I started to read 'Today everything changes', I quickly found out that Andy McNab had problems at school, just like me. After that I could not put the book down. It was very interesting to find out about his school experiences and how life began to change after he joined the army. For me, it was Read Easy that changed my life. This is the favourite of all the books that I have read. I was really excited to meet Andy McNab, when he was giving a talk at a presentation in Stockbridge, Hampshire. After his talk, I met him and he autographed my copy of his book.

Mr Stink had it all, a wife, child and a big house. One day he lost it all, in sad circumstances. He couldn't live in the house anymore, so he packed a bag and walked and walked, never going back. He stayed in one town and the people tried to drive him out but one young girl made friends with him. She decides to try and hide Mr Stink. The book was very sad at the start but funny in places. Just think, one day you may have it all and then you could lose it all.

Depression, dog, decision

I worked as a baker for about ten years. This meant working nights, starting at 5 p.m. and finishing between 2.30 a.m. and 3 a.m. As time went on, I became more and more tired. In the end, I became very depressed and started taking a lot of time off work, so I went to see my doctor for help. The doctor listened to me and prescribed me some anti-depressant tablets. Lorna helped me by putting me in touch with a counsellor at the The Olive Branch in Winchester. I went to two or three sessions there and I was able to talk about how I felt and what I wanted to change especially the loneliness. They said that I was not alone and that many night workers suffered from depression.

After these meetings, I decided to do something to change things, so I left my job in the bakery. I was down and needed help, so my sister who had three dogs, decided to give me one. He was an eight year old Jack Russel called Ben. I enjoyed his company and took him for walks, which got me out of the flat. Ben gave me the hope to change my life. Then I spoke to Read Easy about finding help in applying for jobs. I was introduced to a lady called Sheila. Sheila was kind and helped me write a CV and look for jobs on the computer.

By learning to read and write, I was much more confident in talking to people to get help. One day, while I was walking Ben, I met one of my neighbours and as we were talking , I asked her what she did for a job. She told me that she worked for a company called Apetito, which prepares and delivers meals to vulnerable people. I asked if there were any jobs there and she said that she would ask them. I contacted them and went for an interview. After the interview, they gave me a job and I have been working there ever since. I really enjoy it there.

Apetito, Abbas, Around.

At Apetito, I found a job that I liked. The company is a meals on wheels service. We are based at Itchen Abbas, just outside Winchester. We deliver meals on ten different rounds and I have worked on five of them. It took me a little time to learn the rounds but I know them well now. When I started, two and a half years ago, I only worked on one round, starting at 10 a.m. and finishing at 2.30 p.m. After a while, I took on more kitchen work, cooking the meals for schools during the holidays. In the summer, this meant about three hundred meals a week. I have made a lot of friends here and at the end of the month, we have a tea and cake night, which is always a good laugh. Learning to read and write has really helped me do well in this job.

BBC Radio 5 Live Interview

In February 2021, I had a phone call from Read Easy. They asked me if I would like to go on BBC 5 Live, to answer a few questions about reading, writing and how much being able to do this changed my life. I told Read Easy that I would like to do it and waited for the radio program researcher to contact me. A lady called Jill phoned me and she explained that she contacted people to explain what happened on the show. Jill was a friendly and helpful lady to speak to and after the interview, she texted me to thank me for taking part and wished me good luck for the future. The program was presented by a man called Colin Murray and he would interview me at 10.45 p.m. on April 11th, for about 15 minutes.

A couple of weeks later, John and I met to work out what types of questions I might be asked and how I would answer them. As the time became closer, I was getting more nervous, because this was my first interview on my own. I had been interviewed by Radio Solent with my first coach Lorna. Also I had spoken at a couple meetings, a National Read Easy training conference and the Winchester Writers Society. At the Discovery Centre, I met two students, who talked to me about what technology would help non-readers, which I enjoyed.

April 11th came, it was a Tuesday, so I was working through the day and normally I would be in bed by 9 p.m. In the morning at work, I had a call from a lady called Julie, who asked me if I was still happy to go on the program and I said 'Yes'. She told me that they would call me just before the program started. As the day went on, I became more nervous, thinking about what questions they were going to ask me. I got home from work at about three o'clock and sat there waiting for 10.40 p.m. The time was going very slowly, so I tried to watch some television but there was not anything interesting to watch. In the end, I went to bed and set the alarm 10 p.m. I found it difficult to sleep and just lay there and waited until it was 10 p.m. and then I sat up and put my phone next to me, waiting for the phone to ring.

Finally, at 10.40 p.m. , the phone rang and when I answered it a man spoke to me. He told me to stay on the phone and that he would call me in to the interview. While I was waiting, I could hear the radio show in the background and Colin Murray talked about quite a few people find it hard to read and write. Then he started to talk about football, because Man City had just won the Premiership. He asked me who I supported and I replied that I supported

Portsmouth. This relaxed me a bit and we started to talk about my school days and how not reading and writing affected me and the jobs that I worked in. I described how reading about Andy McNab had motivated me to improve my reading and writing. Another man joined in our conversation, he was introduced as a reading coach. Colin asked what I would tell people, who find reading and writing difficult. I replied that they should not be afraid and ask for help because there are a lot of people out there who will help you, like the coaches at Read Easy, who do amazing work. The interview lasted fifteen minutes and the time went quickly. On the Read Easy UK Facebook page, there is a link to this interview.

ITV Meridian News

In October 2021, I was invited to be interviewed by ITV news at the Discovery Centre in Winchester. I went with Lorna and the Regional Adviser for the South, Michelle, and we were met by an interviewer and cameraman. The interview was about learning to read and write and how it has changed my life.

To begin, I had to pick a book, 'Today Everything Changes' and read two or three pages from it, while I was being filmed. This was repeated four or five times at different angles. Then I was filmed, as the lady asked me her questions. There were about four questions:

- How did I hide not being able to read from friends?

- What was it like at work, when I could not read?

- How did not reading affect my life?

- In what ways has reading changed my life?

Finally, I was filmed walking around and choosing a book to read, signing it out at the desk and walking out of the Discovery Centre. All this filming took about two and a half hours and was edited into a three minute section in the News programme. I really enjoyed the experience and would do it again.

Dear Read Easy,

Thank you very much Read Easy for helping me to read and write. This is the first letter I've ever written.

It has changed the way I do things, my life. It's given me the courage to go out and do different things, not just reading and writing but going out on my own and mixing with the public.

Five or six months ago I would never have done the things I've done, like joining the library, reading newspapers, going on public transport and going to coffee shops and the supermarket. I stayed home before.

I always wanted to read books like my mum. I thought it'd be nice to sit and relax and read books. I started reading but I didn't understand. I'd get to the end of the page and didn't understand so I put it down.

I used to stutter a bit but now I can pronounce long words much more clearer. I've slowed myself down, just like when I'm reading I've slowed myself down. I'm thinking about what I want to say. I used to speak quietly but no one has told me to speak louder for months now.

The other day I went shopping to Sports Direct and bought some t-shirts. I got home, tried them on and 2 didn't fit. So, I took them back. That's the first time I've ever taken something back, and I felt good doing it. I had enough courage to take them back instead of chucking them in the back of the wardrobe. Anything now I would take back if it didn't fit.

I've learned more in the past 6 months than I did at school. If school was like this, I'd be a brain surgeon!

Learning to read has made me more happier, and I'm smiling a lot. It has changed me. The reading is good and has got me to do the rest of it.

Regards
Steve

The Future

I look forward to acting as an Ambassador for Read Easy Winchester and sharing my experiences with other people learning to read and write. I would like to communicate with learners by talking to them on Zoom, about their experiences and mine. With the help of my Read Easy group, my goal is to be a reading coach as well.

Acknowledgements

With special thanks to John McGregor, Lorna & Luke Paviour,
and the whole Read Easy team.

Printed in Great Britain
by Amazon

31861052R00029